I· OF A FRONTIER FAMILY

SQUIRE BOONE was a blacksmith of Berks County, Pennsylvania, who owned a prosperous farm near the frontier village of Reading. The pleasant ringing of hammer on iron made a peaceful music to the goodwife Sarah in the near-by snug log house, where she cooked and wove and washed and spun and managed the eleven husky children that made up the Boone family in the Seventeen Thirties.

From time to time she bundled off two or three of them to the small blab school a mile or so down the road where a crotchety schoolmaster with the aid of a well-worn hickory switch drummed into their tough skins the black arts of reading, 'riting, and 'rithmetic, or as much as they could hold. But they refused really to be hampered by the rules of spelling.

But this time Daniel had the last word, with how she was among her own people, and the Boones and the Bryans would be helping the boys take care of the farm and herself, and himself coming back in the spring with a bale of pelts worth a fortune. This time he was going. So they were saying good-by to the Boones and the Bryans and the Calloways before sunup and waving good-by to Rebecca at the cabin door with the boys, as six of them rode out of the valley in the thick white morning mist.

Finley's cavalcade of six horsemen rode west toward the Watauga River valley, which made a level trail winding between steep shoulders of the mountains. These westward-flowing streams were the only highways through the mountains into the West. To attempt to cross the innumerable ranges would have been a task so slow and tedious as to be almost impossible. Following along the narrow little valley, they soon came out on the south fork of the Holston. This noble river wound through a wider valley of thrilling beauty. They followed down stream to a narrow defile and by stiff climbing passed over the Clinch Mountains and River to the Powell valley.

They were moving through some of the most beautiful country in the world that few white men had ever seen. It was spring, before the leaves were out, and the noble forms of the piling blue ranges stood out in the clear air like sculpture for eternity. When rain and mist slowed down the going, they stretched by the camp fire after the day's march and dried their buckskin leggings, as the shadows danced strangely among the great trees. They were advancing directly onto the mighty wall of the Cumberlands where Finley said they would find a passage through. They climbed easy slopes, stopped, looked back on immense vistas, and went on into new country. Coming down out of the great pass they followed the Cumberland River through wild and savage gorges.

They came now into easy rolling country with low hills where a hunter could range at will. The streams were plentiful and the soil black with richness. Huge black buffalo thundered down to the salt licks or grunted in the juicy canebrakes. The underbrush was thick with game, and they feasted on the fat wild turkey that ran under the horses' feet.

Excited and buoyant they rode northward, coming to the Rockcastle River winding among mountains of fantastic beauty. They kept on north through open country that was a settler's dream of plenty. Soon they were wandering along the fabled banks of the Kentucky. Following the game trails and the wide buffalo streets they discovered the Upper and Lower Blue Licks, the strange mineral springs where the buffalo and deer came eagerly to lick the salty ground.

[3 1]

Having seen no trace of human beings in this Garden of Eden, they forgot the frontier vigilance of Indian fighters, but not for long. As Boone and John Stewart were emerging from a canebrake near the Kentucky River, a dozen Shawnee warriors sprang on them so suddenly that they were captured and bound before they could fire a shot. In this sudden and dismal change of fortune Boone's dauntless spirit rose, and his nonchalance and apparent friendliness made the Indians feel that he was really glad to be captured. After hunting with them for a week, their captors were so completely off guard that Boone and Stewart were able to slip out from their blankets beside the snoring Indians one night and escape to their old camp, only to find that their friends had gone without leaving any sign of when or where. Again Daniel's singing spirit rallied. The two could take care of themselves; they knew all the tricks of the wilderness. So they lived from day to day cautiously spying out the land.

Once from a hilltop they spotted two horsemen riding across an open valley. They lay in ambush looking over their rifle sights. Then with the suddenness of an Indian surprise Daniel recognized his own brother. With masterly woodcraft, Squire Boone and a companion had been able to trail and guess and follow Daniel's path across four hundred miles of trackless mountain wilderness and find him.

Much encouraged and with plenty of supplies, they set about systematic hunting for furs, going off in pairs for the day's hunt and meeting at sundown at their hidden camp. One night, Boone's companion failed to show up. When they could find no trace of him the third man started back for the settlements alone. The two brothers looked at each other across the camp fire that night, alone in a hostile land. They were well-equipped; they were experienced woodsmen. It was foolish to go back without fur bales, and above all the love of the wilderness was in their blood and bones. So they built a hidden cabin against the

cold and trapped and skinned furs all the long white winter. When spring came the fur piles were high and the ammunition low. So they planned for Squire to take back the pelts and Daniel's love to the folks, and he would stay on till Squire returned with more supplies. If it all worked out they would have another long hunt the next year.

Boone stood on a hilltop under a giant walnut tree with his long-barreled rifle across his arm, waving his broad-brimmed hat. He could still see Squire crossing a stream and waving a last good-by before he vanished into the heavy timber. As Boone went back to the cabin a terrible loneliness came over him—a longing for home, Rebecca and the children, friends, and the sound of human voices. He had been a fool not to return with Squire. He cooked his lonesome supper, a strip of venison broiled on the iron ramrod of his rifle. As he sat gazing into the fire he fought a black despair and the primeval nameless fear of darkness that came with the night.

Next day the clear-shining sun rose over the vast land like high-calling trumpets of glory. The splendor and the brightness came upon his spirit like the rushing of mighty wings, and the voice of mighty thunderings: "Enter into a promised land such as no man has known, a new born creation all your own; drink deep, O Daniel, of the mysterious wine of the wilderness."

A new sense of freedom and power possessed him as he ranged over the long hills and followed shrewdly the secret waterways. He was the only freeman in all the western world, like Man himself in the Beginning of Things. Hunter and hunted, he measured his woodcraft against the forest prowlers. Chased to the edge of a high cliff and cornered by Indians, he leaped into a tree-top and so away like the wild rabbit. He hid under waterfalls and swung across streams on wild grapevines. He lay in the canebrake and sang to himself an old Virginia ballad with a rousing refrain. He laughed to think of himself as a jack rabbit dodging

[3 4]

fort was in bad repair. The whole settlement would be utterly unprepared. His hour had come and he was ready. Before dawn he slipped out like a shadow and was gone. Now again he was the hunted fox of the wilderness with the red dogs in close pursuit.

"On the 16th I departed before sunrise in the most secret manner and arrived at Boonesborough on the 20th, after a journey of one hundred and sixty miles, during which I had but one meal." Brief autobiography. How did he know the way all the four days and nights with the Shawnee pack one jump behind?

He was not so young as he used to be but tough and long-winded. When he came at last to the Ohio at full spring flood, he remembered he could not swim. It was the desperate tight spot he had known so often, but the angel of the wilderness showed him a leaky canoe stranded on a sand bar and he made a swift down-stream crossing on the yellow waters to the Kentucky shore that he knew like the back of his hand. Familiar landmarks cheered him. He shot a buffalo and cooked his first meal in four days. He was in sight of Boonesborough. He had kept his rendezvous with destiny.

It was a strange figure that came across the clearing into Boonesborough and said he was Daniel Boone. For weeks they had said Daniel Boone was a goner for sure this time. Even Rebecca's faith had failed and she had returned with the family to the settlements. Boone was sorry, yet glad, too, for she was safe. His brother Israel and Jemima, his beloved daughter who had married Dick Calloway, were there to give him a warm welcome. But it was no wonder Rebecca had gone. Many a husband and father had never come back across the clearing.

The news of the coming Indian raid roused the settlers to action. The neglected log walls were repaired and everything made ready for an attack, the swift short Indian attack with which the borderers were familiar. But weeks passed and no Indians were seen. Then another escaped white man brought in news that

Boone's flight had delayed the Indians. Boone then took a raiding expedition across the Ohio and burned an Indian village, getting back just a few hours ahead of the great war party of over four hundred Indians with some forty French Canadians under the direction of their officer De Quindre.

There were about fifty men and boys, besides the women and children, behind the log stockade when the Indians surrounded the clearing of Boonesborough. Instead of the usual sudden attack, an Indian came out of the woods with a white flag and by calling back and forth arranged for a parley. Every hour of delay meant a nearer hope of reinforcement coming in from Harrodsburg. Three of the defenders met Black Fish, Moluntha, and Catahecassa near the fort for a powwow. There was talk of friendship and peaceful surrender. The chief promised that the whites would be taken safely on horses to Detroit if they surrendered peaceably. There need be no bloodshed if the Americans would agree to abandon the fort.

Boone said he would explain to his people and in two days give an answer. He was glad to find that the Indians had heard from a white captive that there were several hundred defenders in the fort. The Indians believed their offer of safety was sure to be accepted.

Inside the fort the chances were talked over and argued and weighed after the democratic way of the backwoods. The odds were ten to one and worse against defense, and not a man, woman, or child would be spared if—But the tough cantankerous spirit of the frontier urged: "Go ahead or bust." They would not have been where they were if they had not been stubborn survivors of a rough, tough, restless race who lived and died in their own independent way by the rifle, the ax, the Bible, and the plow. So they sent back the eagle's answer: "No surrender," the answer of the sassy two-year-old baby democracy, the answer of Man the Unconquerable to the hosts of darkness—"No surrender."

[5 9]

The iron-faced chiefs and the ornery Frenchman De Quindre took the answer grimly back to their council, while the settlers got in their cows, corn, and water from the spring without interference from the Indians. The next move was an Indian trick which was perfectly transparent to Boone, but he took the chances of playing it to win time.

The Indians proposed a grand council of nine on each side to sign a treaty of peace, after which they would depart, they said, like lambs. The council sat under the sycamore trees within rifle shot of the fort. At a wave of the hat from the delegates the riflemen in the fort were to open fire and cover the nine men's dash back when trouble started.

All day they sat in the shade and smoked, talked, and ate while a fancy treaty of peace, including a sworn allegiance to the British Crown, was agreed on, to be signed tomorrow at the same place. In the night an ambush of Indians was set around the treaty tree. The next day when the nine appeared from the fort, Black Fish met them with eighteen powerful young braves. After the signing came the two-to-one hand-shaking. Two Indians grabbed for each white man and a mob jumped from the laurel to finish the job. Then the nine Kentucky wildcats let loose with teeth and claws, and the fur flew. Shooting began and the nine raced for the fort. They had won the first round.

Next day there was a great hubbub in the forest, bugles blowing and orders for retreat bawled out, and the pack horses were seen crossing the river at the ford. But the old border fox in the fort was not fooled. The gates of Boonesborough remained shut and the Indian trick failed. The real danger was an Indian rush on the gates under a heavy fire from all sides. This was what kept the riflemen waiting and watching at the portholes day and night.

But to charge across the clearing under the fire of Kentucky rifles was so contrary to the Indian way of fighting that all of DeQuindre's urging for a mass

attack was useless. Instead, the savages remained under cover of the woods, firing continuously. Day and night under the heavy encircling fire of the enemy, the riflemen stuck to their posts, blazing away whenever an inch of Indian hide was exposed to view. The women passed out the scant rations and scarce water, loaded guns when the firing was fast, molded bullets, comforted the children, and prayed the prayers of the pioneer faith. Each slow day under the burning sun was an eternity; each night they thanked the God of their Fathers that some protecting angel had kept the gates.

the Virginia Assembly there was a big hurrah and shouting and speechifying for Colonel Boone. Wasn't he the only candidate that could write and could do surveying? So the Boones left the valley to go down to Richmond to the Assembly where Daniel had been twice before, the first time being the occasion of his remarkable capture by the British cavalrymen. The frontier colonel listened gravely to the elegant speechifying in the Virginia Assembly and voted for anything that benefited the folks back in Kanawha.

[8 3]

But before long Boone was moving up the Kanawha valley farther and farther away from the settlements on hunting trips and sometimes riding down to the river towns to trade furs. Occasionally he did surveying jobs for a grabbing land company or a lone settler.

To the new generations sweeping on he was like a page out of the past, a patriarchal figure around whom hung fantastic legends and romance. He was pointed out to strangers when he rode into the ragged streets of a sprawling boom-town. Being a curiosity annoyed him and he grew more and more uncomfortable in the raw new undergrowth of humanity sprouting up so rankly on the old hunting- and battlegrounds that were full of memories.

He was hearing stories about the rich hunting-grounds beyond the Mississippi—stories that reminded him of Finley, that stirred the same call to be moving on. It was like his lost youth calling again when young Daniel Morgan Boone came and told the old hunter that he was going with a party of settlers into the Spanish country, down the Ohio to St. Louis. The colonel was excited and pleased. Rebecca no longer protested. She had followed the many trails with a vast patience tempered by the long hard years.

Word at last came back from young Daniel that the Kentucky settlers had been granted fat farms on Femme Osage Creek about forty miles from St. Louis and that the hunting was fine. Rebecca saw it coming. She knew nothing could keep the older Daniel from going. He was full of the old enthusiasm, was happy again and busy in preparation. So the word got around that on such a day Colonel Boone was starting down to the river for the fabulous mysterious West. The Kanawha folk around Charleston gathered for a big farewell and barbecue and gave the Boones a whooping good-by as they rode down the valley. They loaded his best Kentucky horses and cows, his favorite hounds on the flatboats until it seemed very much like an amiable Noah's Ark. With some careful poling they

[84]

got out into the Ohio where the spring floods had speeded up the current and the long wooden sweeps held her in the channel.

No wonder Boone felt he was entering upon the happiest time of his life since his first trip into Kentucky. The voyage down the peaceful winding river was like a beautiful dream. When they pulled up at the little river towns everybody turned out to cheer and welcome them and beg them to stay longer. It filled the old man's heart with joy to feel that he was loved and honored by the people he had known so well. They drifted by the quiet shores he had known in times of danger, and past the mouths of rivers with silver-sounding names—Scioto, Miami, Wabash, Kaskaskia. On the left were the rivers of the promised land whose secret sources in the Cumberland Mountains he had sought out in the long ago, the Licking, Kentucky, Greene, Cumberland, Tennessee.

He was going west again, floating down the ample river in the beautiful Ohio spring, following the American dream.

V · LONG AFTERNOON

AT LAST the river voyage was ended and the Boones were crossing the Mississippi, the Father of Waters, into the little easy-going town of St. Louis. Boone was treading on the same spot where the great La Salle had built the first fort so long ago. He, too, had been a wilderness explorer of the farthest reaches, with his head full of great visions for a French empire of the Mississippi. And even before La Salle, at a point farther down the river, on a moonless night they had dropped into the dark waters the worn body of another seeker of far horizons, the Spaniard De Soto.